cat

кошка

rabbit

кролик

dog

собака

chick

цыпленок

duck

утка

sheep

овца

goat

коза

pig

свинья

donkey

осёл

horse

лошадь

cow

корова

mouse

мышь

bat

летучая мышь

bee

пчела

spider

паук

fox

лиса

deer

олень

squirrel

белка

hedgehog

ёж

owl

сова

frog

лягушка

snake
змея

racoon

енот

parrot

попугай

toucan

тукан

alligator

аллигатор

sea turtle

морская черепаха

flamingo

фламинго

penguin

пингвин

crab

**краб

jellyfish

медуза

seal

тюлень

shark

акула

whale

кит

orca

косатка

starfish

морская звезда

rhinoceros

носорог

panda

панда

monkey

обезьяна

lion

лев

tiger

тигр

elephant

слон